Conten

WHAT ARE WE GOING TO LEARN?

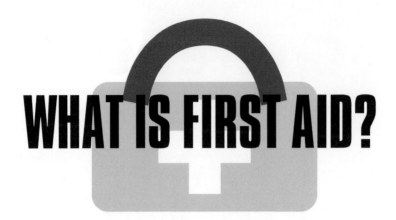

WHAT IS FIRST AID?

FIRST AID IS HELP YOU CAN GIVE TO SOMEONE WHO IS SICK OR INJURED BEFORE THE AMBULANCE ARRIVES.

WHAT IS THE JOB OF A FIRST AIDER?

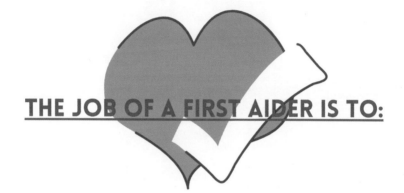

THE JOB OF A FIRST AIDER IS TO:

> **KEEP YOURSELF AND THE CASUALTY SAFE**

> **STOP ANYONE GETTING ANY FURTHER INJURIES;**

> **GET HELP FROM THE EMERGENCY SERVICES IF NEEDED**

> **QUICKLY AND SAFELY TREAT ANY INJURIES;**

IMPORTANT THINGS TO KNOW ABOUT FIRST AID

SAFETY

BEFORE YOU HELP SOMEONE INJURED OR SICK, MAKE SURE IT IS SAFE TO DO SO.

TALKING TO YOUR CASUALTY

YOU SHOULD ASK EASY QUESTIONS SUCH AS:

- WHERE DOES IT HURT?
- HOW ARE YOU FEELING?
- HOW DID IT HAPPEN?
- DO YOU HAVE YOUR OWN MEDICINE THAT I CAN GET FOR YOU?

IF SOMEONE IS INJURED OR UNWELL, YOU SHOULD CALL FOR AN AMBULANCE

CALLING FOR AN AMBULANCE

IT IS IMPORTANT YOU KNOW THE ADDRESS OF WHERE YOU ARE!

WHAT HAS HAPPENED?

WHAT IS WRONG WITH YOUR CASUALTY?

WHERE ARE YOU?

999 or 112

Super Saver

AN AMBULANCE CAN TAKE THE INJURED PERSON TO HOSPITAL WHERE THEY WILL GET HELP FROM A DOCTOR OR A NURSE.

WHAT IS THE FIRST THING YOU SHOULD DO WHEN YOU SEE SOMEONE WHO NEEDS FIRST AID?

YOU SHOULD CHECK THE AREA FOR ANY DANGERS OR HAZARDS WHICH COULD HURT YOU OR THE CASUALTY

WHICH TWO TELEPHONE NUMBERS CAN YOU CALL FOR EMERGENCY HELP?

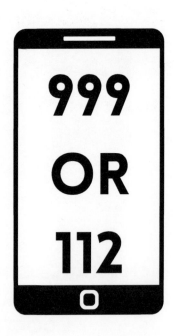

999 OR 112

WHATS IN A FIRST AID KIT?

THERE ARE MANY DIFFERENT SIZES AND TYPES OF FIRST AID KITS. EVERY HOME SHOULD HAVE ONE.

IMPORTANT: (THESE ARE JUST SOME ITEMS IN A FIRST AID KIT.)

CIRCLE WHAT YOU THINK IS CORRECT.

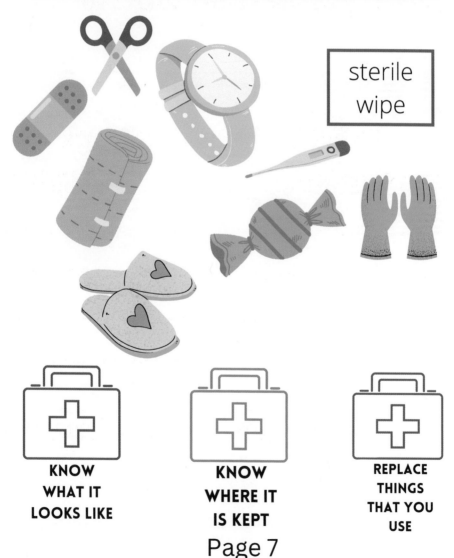

sterile wipe

| KNOW WHAT IT LOOKS LIKE | KNOW WHERE IT IS KEPT | REPLACE THINGS THAT YOU USE |

FIRST AID

WORDSEARCH

HINT: 2 ARE MISSING

```
F  R  A  C  T  U  R  E  B  Z
M  P  L  A  S  T  E  R  L  U
E  K  W  N  P  I  C  L  O  T
D  B  K  S  R  J  O  Q  O  L
I  U  I  R  A  H  V  C  D  L
C  V  T  A  I  C  E  R  S  Z
I  T  H  E  N  I  R  O  W  R
N  B  T  U  R  E  Y  Y  F  Z
E  U  P  B  A  N  D  A  G  E
```

Plaster	Fracture	CPR
Recovery	Clot	Airway
Sprain	Blood	Kit
Bandage	Ice	Medicine

COLOURING PAGE

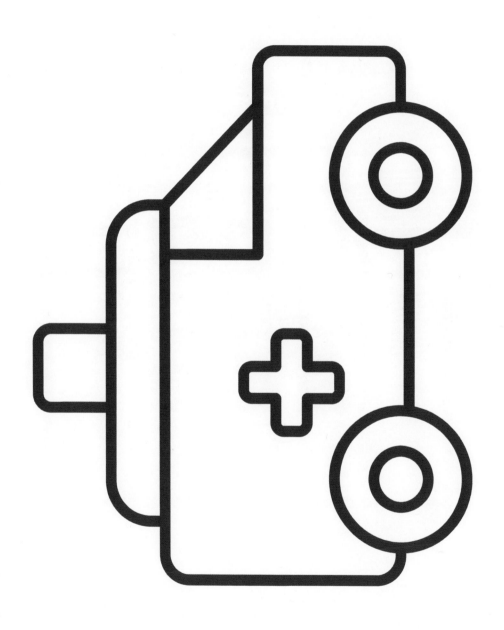

COLOURING PAGE

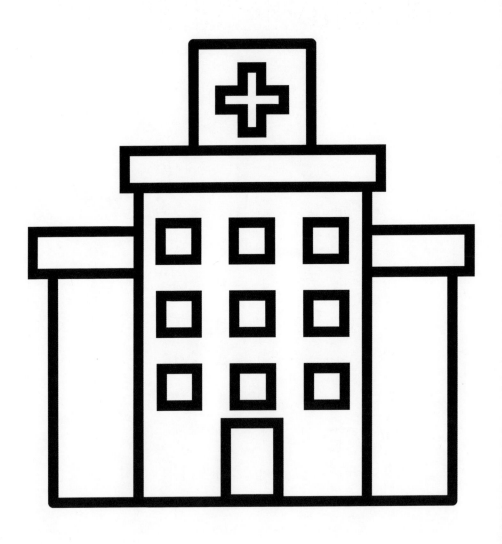

COLOURING PAGE

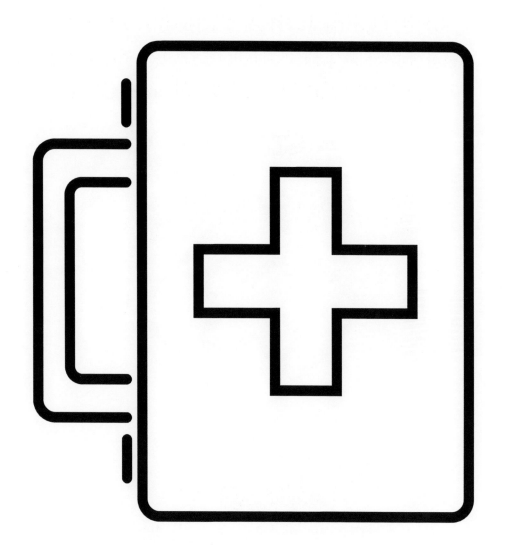

COLOURING PAGE

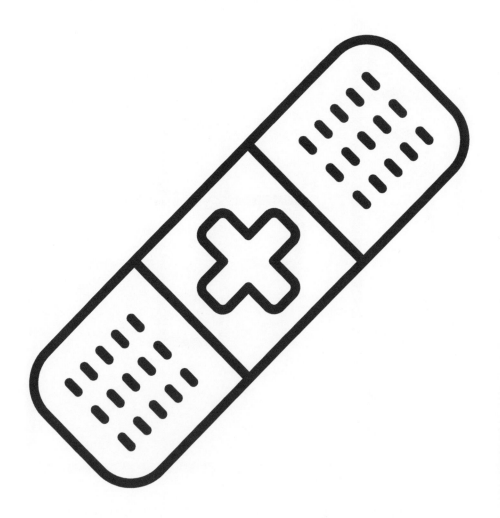

COLOURING PAGE

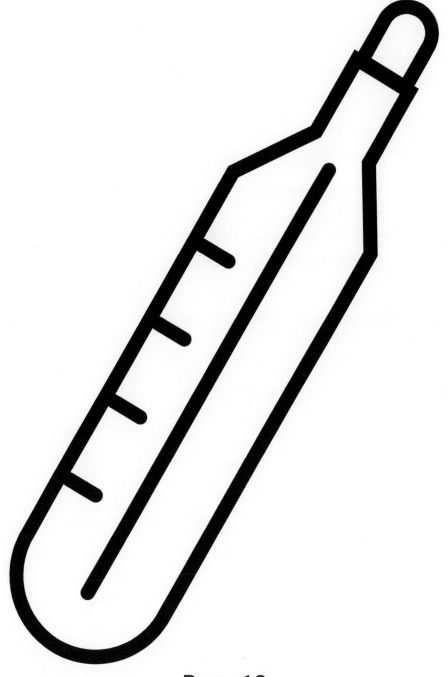

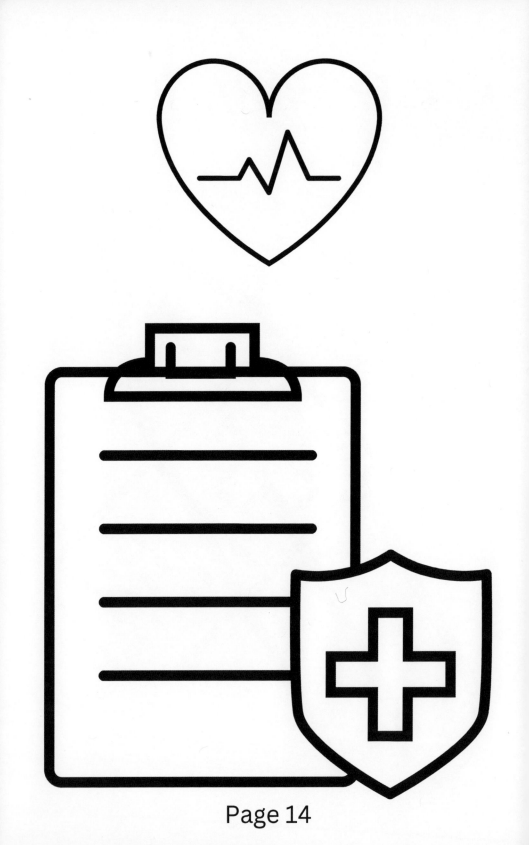

DR ABC

D   IS FOR DANGER.

R   IS FOR RESPONSE.

A   IS FOR AIRWAY.

B   IS FOR BREATHING.

C   IS FOR CIRCULATION..

D: DANGER

BEFORE YOU OFFER HELP, STOP AND LOOK AROUND FOR ANY DANGERS

WHAT DANGERS MIGHT BE PRESENT?

HOW CAN YOU CHECK THAT AN AREA IS SAFE?

WHAT SHOULD YOU DO IF YOU SPOT A DANGER WHICH COULD HURT YOU IF YOU TRY TO HELP THE CASUALTY?

CIRCLE THE 14 DANGERS

Page 18

SHOUT FOR HELP

IF YOU ARE ON YOUR OWN, DON'T BE AFRAID TO SHOUT FOR HELP!

A HELPER COULD GET THE FIRST AID KIT, OR CALL FOR AN AMBULANCE.

IT'S IMPORTANT TO ALWAYS REMAIN CALM.

R: RESPONSE

NOW THE AREA IS SAFE, YOU CAN GO TO THE CASUALTY AND CHECK TO SEE HOW THEY ARE.

IF THEY ARE TALKING TO YOU, THEN YOU KNOW THEY ARE BREATHING AND THEY ARE RESPONDING TO YOU

HOWEVER, IF THEY ARE NOT TALKING TO YOU, YOU CAN GENTLY SHAKE THEIR SHOULDERS AND ASK THEM LOUDLY

"ARE YOU ALRIGHT?"

KNEEL NEXT TO THEIR CHEST AND GENTLY SHAKE THEIR SHOULDERS ASKING, "WHAT HAS HAPPENED?" OR "OPEN YOUR EYES."
IF THE CASUALTY OPENS THEIR EYES OR TRIES TO ANSWER YOU, THEY ARE RESPONSIVE.

IF THEY DO NOT RESPOND TO YOU, THEY ARE UNRESPONSIVE AND NEED TO BE TREATED AS QUICKLY AS POSSIBLE.

A: AIRWAY

NEXT, YOU NEED TO CHECK THAT THE CASUALTY'S AIRWAY IS OPEN AND CLEAR.

IF THEY TALK TO YOU, THEIR AIRWAY IS OPEN AND CLEAR.

IF THEY DO NOT RESPOND TO YOU, ASK SOMEONE TO CALL FOR HELP WHILE YOU OPEN THEIR AIRWAY

DO THIS BY PLACING ONE HAND ON THEIR FOREHEAD AND GENTLY TILTING THEIR HEAD BACK. USE TWO FINGERS FROM THE OTHER HAND TO LIFT THEIR CHIN TO OPEN THEIR AIRWAY.

B: BREATHING

YOU NOW NEED TO CHECK TO SEE IF THE CASUALTY IS BREATHING NORMALLY.

LOOK FOR CHEST MOVEMENT

↓

LISTEN AT THEIR MOUTH FOR BREATH SOUNDS

↓

FEEL FOR AIR ON YOUR CHEEK

IF THEY ARE UNRESPONSIVE AND NOT BREATHING NORMALLY, YOU NEED TO CALL 999 OR 112 FOR EMERGENCY HELP STRAIGHT AWAY.

IF THEY DID NOT RESPOND TO YOU BUT ARE BREATHING NORMALLY, PLACE THEM IN THE RECOVERY POSITION, CALL FOR EMERGENCY HELP AND KEEP MONITORING THEM UNTIL EMERGENCY HELP ARRIVES

C IS FOR CPR
(IF NOT BREATHING)

IF YOUR CASUALTY IS NOT BREATHING NORMALLY, YOU SHOULD FIRST CALL 999 AND ASK FOR AN AMBULANCE.

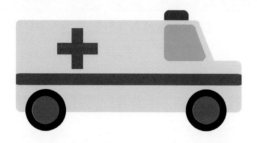

IF YOUR CASUALTY IS BREATHING NORMALLY, YOU SHOULD PLACE YOUR CASUALTY IN THE RECOVERY POSITION

CPR PROCEDURE
(FOR ADULTS)

AS SOON AS YOU HAVE ESTABLISHED THAT YOUR CASUALTY IS NOT BREATHING NORMALLY, YOU MUST CALL FOR AN AMBULANCE IMMEDIATELY BEFORE YOU COMMENCE CPR

START WITH 30 CHEST COMPRESSIONS

THE HEEL OF ONE HAND MUST BE PLACED IN THE CENTRE OF THE CHEST – (THE BOTTOM HALF OF THE STERNUM OR BREASTBONE)

PLACE YOUR OTHER HAND ON TOP AND CLASP THEM TOGETHER WITH YOUR ARMS LOCKED STRAIGHT

⬇

AFTER 30 CHEST COMPRESSIONS, GIVE YOUR CASUALTY   2 RESCUE BREATHS THE RECOGNISED METHODS FOR THIS ACTION ARE EITHER   BY MOUTH TO MOUTH OR MOUTH TO NOSE

IT IS IMPORTANT TO REMEMBER CPR PROCEDURES ARE DIFFERENT FOR CHILDREN AND BABIES

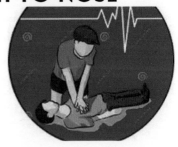

C: CIRCULATION

(IF THEY ARE BREATHING)

ONCE YOU ARE SURE THAT THE CASUALTY IS BREATHING NORMALLY, YOU NEED TO LOOK AND CHECK FOR ANY SIGNS OF SEVERE BLEEDING.

IF THEY ARE BLEEDING SEVERELY, YOU WILL NEED TO TRY TO CONTROL AND TREAT THE BLEEDING.

DO THIS BY PUTTING PRESSURE ON THE WOUND. CALL 999 OR 112 FOR EMERGENCY HELP.

IF THEY ARE UNRESPONSIVE AND BREATHING NORMALLY, PUT THEM IN THE RECOVERY POSITION AND CALL 999 OR 112 FOR EMERGENCY HELP. YOU CAN CHECK FOR SEVERE BLEEDING WHILE YOU WAIT FOR THE EMERGENCY HELP TO ARRIVE.

RECOVERY POSITION

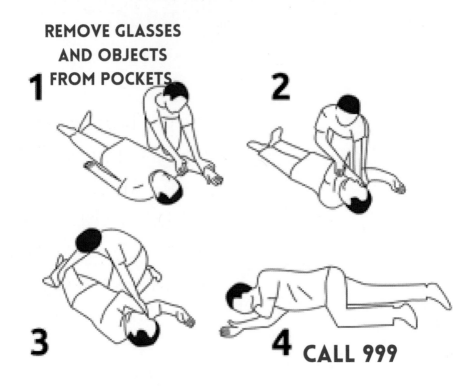

REMOVE GLASSES AND OBJECTS FROM POCKETS

1

2

3

4 CALL 999

NOW YOU HAVE PLACED THEM IN THE RECOVERY POSITION, YOU MUST NOW CALL FOR AN AMBULANCE IF YOU HAVEN'T ALREADY DONE SO

KEEP THEM WARM BY PLACING A COAT OR BLANKET OVER THEM. KEEP TALKING TO THEM.

MAKE SURE THEY ARE STILL BREATHING NORMALLY AND WAIT FOR THE AMBULANCE TO ARRIVE.

HELP AT HOME ACTIVITY SHEET

ADD YOUR NAME, ADDRESS AND DETAILS TO THE
CONTACT CARD AND KEEP IT IN A SAFE PLACE IN CASE OF
EMERGENCY. THERE IS ALSO SPACE FOR YOU TO ADD
ANOTHER ADDRESS. CHOOSE A PLACE THAT YOU SPEND
A LOT OF TIME WHEN YOU ARE NOT AT HOME. THIS
COULD BE A GRANDPARENT'S HOUSE, A FRIEND'S HOUSE
OR A PLACE IN YOUR LOCAL AREA.

EMERGENCY CONTACT DETAILS

ADDRESS 1:

_____

_____

_____

_____

POST CODE: ·

ADDRESS 2:

_____

_____

_____

_____

POST CODE: ·

FANTASTIC FIRST AID HELPER

This is Certificate is rewarded to:

_____

AWARDED BY: _____ DATE: _____

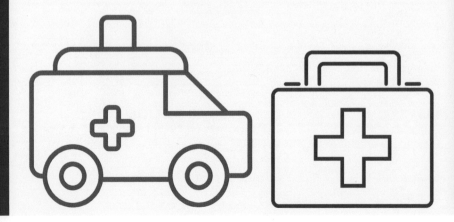

WHATS IN A FIRST AID KIT?

THERE ARE MANY DIFFERENT SIZES AND TYPES OF FIRST AID KITS.

CIRCLE WHAT YOU THINK IS CORRECT.

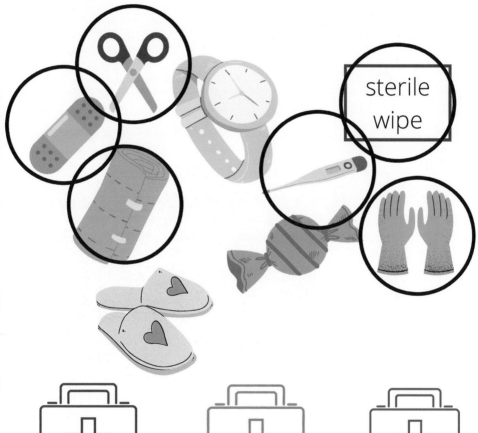

sterile wipe

KNOW WHAT IT LOOKS LIKE

KNOW WHERE IT IS KEPT

REPLACE THINGS THAT YOU USE

FIRST AID
WORDSEARCH

HINT: 2 ARE MISSING

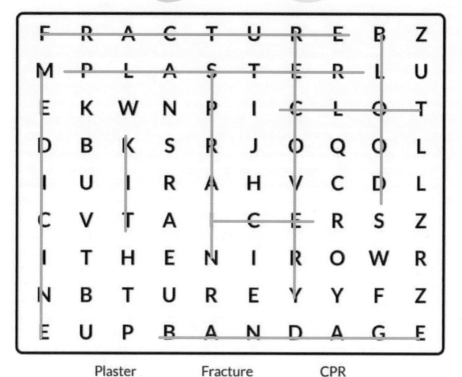

```
F R A C T U R E B Z
M M P L A S T E R L U
E K W N P I C L O T
D B K S R J O Q O L
I U I R A H V C D L
C V T A C E R S Z
I T H E N I R O W R
N B T U R E Y Y F Z
E U P B A N D A G E
```

Plaster	Fracture	CPR
Recovery	Clot	Airway
Sprain	Blood	Kit
Bandage	Ice	Medicine

Printed in Great Britain
by Amazon